MW00366679

Vnde sit potio cōsolo [illegible]
lidatiua. & genera[illegible]
ns canalis et seis. [illegible]
pt qm de generacia: [illegible]
qz uehiculū ē alioꝝ. tenet iste liber et
uno distēperet. et usqz ad cōsūpcōem tercie
bulliat. deinde [illegible] ad quantitatē p[illegible]
et iterum usqz ad cōsūpcōem tercie p[illegible]
[illegible] sic fiat usqz p [illegible] decoccōem et
[illegible] depōt et usui reseruet. Ista potio
[illegible] pacientes ter in die. nulla certa [illegible]
[illegible]: sz solū [illegible] rubei [illegible]
[illegible] supponat. Vl s: Recipe
[illegible] absinthij. pigle. bu
[illegible] [illegible] det uulnerato.

[illegible] dig
[illegible]
[illegible]
[illegible]
uidet singl[illegible]
Si uō [illegible]
[illegible] et p[illegible]
[illegible]
[illegible]
[illegible] uidet
[illegible] salsa.
[illegible]
[illegible]
[illegible]
[illegible]

Et sanguis leporis illinitus : non solum sa-
phelid impetigines et serpigines pur-
ificat. Venter leporis delectat in con-
[illegible] die in [illegible] de ped-
icoribus. Nota quod sanguis ped[illegible] est
[illegible] in isto [illegible]
[illegible]

[illegible] mes deus amenes
e lavez fra [illegible]

WHAT THE APOTHECARY ORDERED

Published in Great Britain in 2015 by Old House books & maps
c/o Osprey Publishing, PO Box 883, Oxford OX2 9PH, UK.
c/o Osprey Publishing, PO Box 3985, New York, NY 10185-3985, USA.
Website: www.oldhousebooks.co.uk

© 2014 Old House

All rights reserved. Apart from any fair dealing for the purpose of private study, research, criticism or review, as permitted under the Copyright, Designs and Patents Act, 1988, no part of this publication may be reproduced, stored in a retrieval system, or transmitted in any form or by any means, electronic, electrical, chemical, mechanical, optical, photocopying, recording or otherwise, without the prior written permission of the copyright owner. Enquiries should be addressed to the Publishers. Every attempt has been made by the Publishers to secure the appropriate permissions for materials reproduced in this book. If there has been any oversight we will be happy to rectify the situation and a written submission should be made to the Publishers.

A CIP catalogue record for this book is available from the British Library.

ISBN-13: 978 1 90840 286 8

Compiled by Caroline Rance.

Images are acknowledged as follows:
The Advertising Archives / The Bridgeman Art Library, pages 70, 87 and 165; Bibliotheque des Arts Decoratifs, Paris, France / Archives Charmet / The Bridgeman Art Library, page 60; Boston Public Library, pages 73 and 105; British Library Images, pages 24, 141, 161 and 174; De Agostini Picture Library / G. Dagli Orti / The Bridgeman Art Library, page 120; Paul Getty Museum, page 133; Lewis Walpole Library, pages 65 and 152; Library of Congress, pages 50, 78, 128 and 158; Mary Evans, page 8; National Library of Medicine, pages 98, 102, 137; Victoria & Albert Museum, London, UK / The Bridgeman Art Library, pages 20 and 148; Wellcome Collection Images, pages 11, 13, 16, 23, 29, 30, 43, 44, 49, 53, 56, 74, 77, 81, 84, 89, 92, 101, 106, 109, 112, 116, 134, 138, 142, 162, 168, 171, 172 and 176.

All other images are from the collection of the editor.

Printed in China through World Print Ltd.

15 16 17 18 19 11 10 9 8 7 6 5 4 3 2

CONTENTS

A NOTE FROM THE EDITOR

Beware, oh faint of heart, for I speak not of gentle therapy and kindly bedside manner! This humble work is intended for the stalwart of stomach and the robust of sensibility; those who can cast squeamishness aside and relish stories of a less than delicate nature.

Throughout history, the human race's determination to survive has taken some ingenious and dangerous turns. This book comprises a selection of the more curious health advice of the past 2,000 years, drawing on the work of many practitioners of varying states of qualification. It is to be acknowledged, of course, that the remedies of the past were not universally poisonous or revolting – common sense, acute observation and a knowledge of the properties of herbs and minerals have all played their part. In the present volume, however, we are concerned only with the odd, the entertaining and the distinctly unappealing.

No remedy contained herein should be seen as the standard treatment used by 'the Victorians' or 'the Anglo-Saxons' or anybody else. At various periods of history, people facing illness and injury have been active participants in their search for recovery, often holding the power in their relationships with practitioners

and trying many treatments until time (or death) brought relief. The advice herein represents only some of those choices. It was not intended to hurt or disgust, but to have a positive effect, and with this in mind we would be wise to see the remedies not as the product of ignorance but of invention.

As the cures detailed in the following pages are gathered from numerous works originating in different times and places, you will encounter inconsistencies of spelling and unexpected punctuation. I feel it is not my place to 'correct' language that was accurate in the context of its time, and shall leave the writers to speak in their own voices. Some were educated at the finest European universities; some gathered together the knowledge relied upon within their communities. And, of course, there were (as there are now) some keen to make a fast buck from people's very real health and beauty anxieties.

It is my duty as a responsible editor to warn you not to try these remedies at home (or, indeed, anywhere else). If you are under the weather, please consult your doctor or pharmacist.

Yet on that note, I must impart a final warning: think not that the twenty-first century provides you with a shield against

questionable cures! We are indeed fortunate in the effective drugs and procedures now available, but they are not to be taken for granted. There are still those among us who propagate scaremongering stories and pretended miracle cures; those who spend thousands on untested potions; those who forget to finish their antibiotics because they feel a bit better. At the very moment you are reading this book, charlatans are preying on false hopes, bacteria are evolving drug resistance, and human nature remains credulous enough to keep strange remedies alive.

Above all, no matter what century we live in, we are stalked by that grim physician who relieves our pains once and for all – DEATH! All who gave or took the advice contained in this book are now gone from this world. And we would do well to remember that for all our technologies and pharmaceuticals, we are destined to follow.

As they are, so shall we be. Medicine or no medicine.

Yours morbidly,

The Editor

Here you may be Cured-

CHAPTER

I

DESPERATE REMEDIES

Of annoying ailments and deadly diseases

BLEEDING AT THE NOSE

Father Schott the Jesuit says, that to stop a Bleeding at the Nose, you need only to hold to the Nose the Dung of an Ass very hot, wrap'd up in an Handkerchief, upon the plea that the Smell will presently stop it. Wecher did the same with Hogs Dung very hot done up in fine Taffeta, and put into the nose.

– *Recreations Mathematical and Physical,* 1708

Dr. RICHARD ROCK's Tincture for Curing the TEETH.

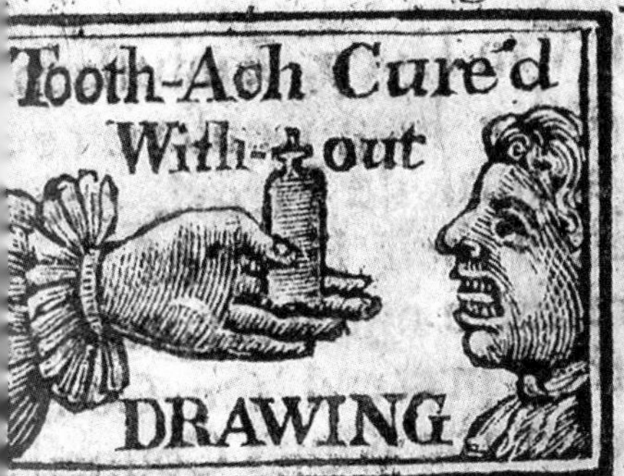

WHICH makes the fouleſt Teeth moſt beautifully white at once or twice uſing; and ſpeedily cures all Diſorders of the Gums or Teeth whatever. It gives immediate Eaſe in the moſt violent Pain, and prevents its Return; it preſerves the Teeth from growing rotten, and faſtens thoſe that are looſe; it erfectly cures the Scurvy in the Gums, cauſing them to grow up o the Teeth again to Admiration, and is exceeding good for an ll-ſcented Breath.

It is likewiſe a moſt excellent Beautifier of the Face, that infalibly kills Worms, takes away Freckles, Spots, Wrinkles, Pits or Marks of the Small Pox, &c. and ſpeedily clears, plumps, Nouriſhes and whitens the Skin to a Miracle. To be had at the Hand and Face near Black-Fryars Stairs, at Mr. Bagſhaw's at the Piazza, Billingſgate, at Mr. Barr's, a Stocking-maker by Leiceſter-Gate, Leiceſter-Fields, at Mr. Brooks's the Eſſex Serpent in Kingſtreet, Covent Garden, and at the Rainbow Coffee-Houſe at Fleet-Bridge. Price One Shilling, with Directions.

N. B. At the ſame Places is to be had the Chymical Liquor for Curing the ITCH. Price 1 s. 6 d. the Bottle, with Directions. Likewiſe Pitcarn's Purging Elixir. Price 1 s. the Bottle, with Directions.

N. B, Advice will be given gratis, in moſt difficult Diſtempers, from One o' Clock till Five and from Eight till Ten at Night.

THE ANTI-PESTILENTIAL QUILT

This quilt must be worn at the Pit of the Stomach, next the Skin; which may easily be contrived by hanging it over the Neck with a Ribband or Fillet, and tying it close to the Stomach by another Ribband going round the Body.

Care must be taken to pull off the Quilt every Week, and to dry it gradually by the Fire; not too near, but sufficiently so that the Heat may draw from it all the Moisture which it shall have attracted from the Body by Insensible Perspiration.

It is by this insensible Perspiration, effected by the Quilt, that the Blood purges itself of malignant Humours, the Retention of which often occasions melancholy Diseases, and especially the Small Pox.

– *Manner of Wearing the Anti-Pestilential Quilt*, c. 1780

All In Search of Health
Should Wear Harness'
"Electropathic"
Belt.
For Suffering Men & Women.
For Ladies
For Gentlemen

SNEEZING

Sneezing, provoked by a feather, relieves heaviness in the head; it is said too, that to touch the nostrils of a mule with the lips, will arrest sneezing and hiccup.

– Pliny the Elder, *The Natural History*, c. AD 77–79

FOR THE AGUE

A small living spider should be rolled up in a cobweb, then put into a lump of butter and eaten while the fit is on. Pills, also, may be made of the cobwebs in which the eggs remain, and taken daily for three days; after which time it would be dangerous to continue the treatment.

– *Ancient Cures, Charms and Usages of Ireland,* 1890

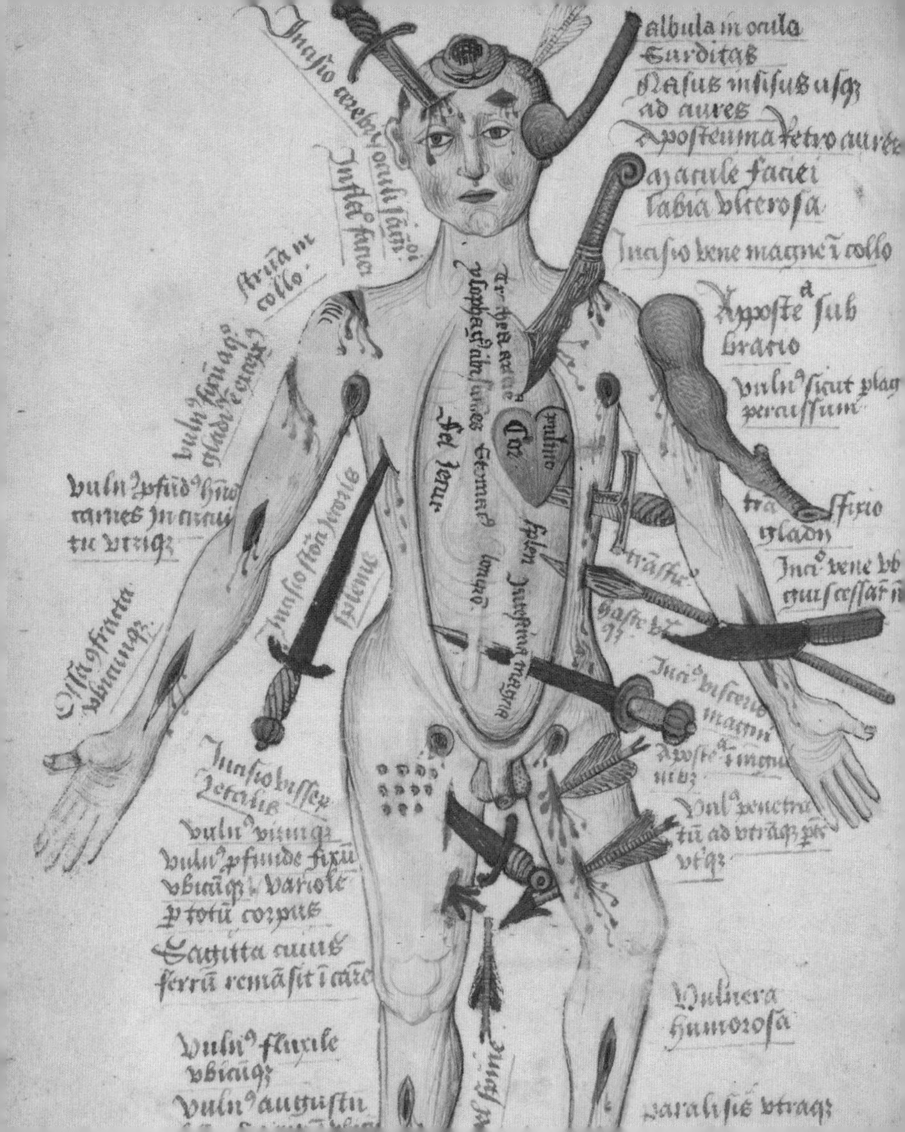

Incisio cerebri
albula in oculo
Surditas
Nasus incisus usque ad aures
Apostema retro aures
macule faciei
labia ulcerosa
Incisio oculi faciei
Inflatio faciei
Incisio vene magne in collo
struma in collo
Trachea arteria
ysophagus cum sanie
Aposte[a] sub brachio
vulnus furiag gladii & enis
vulnus sicut plaga percussum
Cor
pulmo
Fel
Iecur
Stomachus
vulnus profundum hinc carnes in trauma utrique
transfixio gladii
Incisio stomachi
Incisio splenis
splen
longus
Intestina magna
Inci[o] vene ubi non cessat
trasfixio
Ossa fracta ubicumque
basse vulnus
Inci[o] visceris magni
Aposte[a] in membris
Incisio vesice letalis
vulnus utrumque
Vulnus penetrativum ad utraque partes utique
vulnus profunde fixum ubicumque Variole per totum corpus
Sagitta cuius ferrum remansit in carne
Vulnera humorosa
Vulnus fluxile ubicumque
Vulnus augustum
paralisis utraque

TO STANCH THE BLEEDING OF A WOUND

Take a Hounds turd, and lay that on a hot coal, and binde it thereto, and that shall stanch bleeding, or else bruise a long Worm, and make a powder of it, and cast it on the wound, or take the ear of a Hare and make a powder thereof, and cast that on the wound, and that will stanch bleeding.

– *A Choice Manual*, 1653

FOR THE EPILEPSY

A Fit may be thus prevented: Let the Patient have ready a Piece of Metal as broad as he is able to contain between his Teeth, when his Jaws are stretched to the utmost. As soon as he feels the first Symptom, let him take the Piece of Metal, and opening his Teeth as wide as he can, put it between them, that his Jaws may be kept at their utmost stretch for some Time. This will restore him in about Half a Minute, and prevent the Fit for that Time.

– *The Family Guide to Health*, 1767

HOW TO KNOW THE KING'S EVIL

Take a ground-worm and lay it alive upon the place grieved, then take a green Dock-leaf or two, and lay them upon the worm, and then binde the same about the neck of the Patient at night when he goes to bed, and in the morning when he riseth take it off again, and if it be the Kings-evil the worm will be turned into powder or dust, or else he will be and remain dead in his own former form.

– *The Poor Man's Physician and Chyrurgion*, 1656

AN OCCASIONAL DRAUGHT TO PROMOTE APPETITE

Take of sulphuric acid five drops, in a glass of cold water.

– *The Medical Adviser, or, Guide to Health and Long Life*, 1824

AGAINST VENOM

So the Arse of a Hen plucked bare, and applyed to the biting of a viper, freeth the body from venome, and the Hen swells, and if not cured, dies sooner than if she had been struck with the viper.

– *Medicina magnetica,* 1656

vous savoir des orine

A MEDICINE FOR A DEAF AND PAINED EAR

Take a Hedgehog and flay him and rost him, and let the Patient put some of the grease or fat that comes from him into his ear, and he will recover his hearing in a short space.

– *The Poor Man's Physician and Chyrurgion*, 1656

REMEDY FOR A DISEASE GENERALLY CALLED THE 'SHINGLES AROUND THE WAIST'

Rub the parts affected with the Oil of Cedar, morning and night, for about two days. If this produces a burning pain that can be no longer borne, the blood of a black cat may be rubbed on twice a day, until cured.

The rubbing on of cat's blood may seem ridiculous in the eyes of some, but let them try it, and perhaps their ridicule will cease, when forced to admit that there exist remedies in nature for the cure of diseases, the cause of which we are not able to explain. Whether the blood of a white or brown cat will answer the same purpose or not, and why not, is not my purpose to explain here; and any one anxious to know may search the mystery himself. I have tried the above; it has fully answered its purpose in giving relief and performing a final cure, and what experience has taught me is good, I can conscientiously recommend to others; whether they laugh at it or not is of little difference to me.

– *The Poor Man's Friend*, 1847

A HUMAN BITE

The human bite is also looked upon as one of the most dangerous of all. The proper remedy for it is human ear-wax: a thing that we must not be surprised at, seeing that, if applied immediately, it is a cure for the stings of scorpions even, and serpents. The best, however, for this purpose, is that taken from the ears of the wounded person.

– Pliny the Elder, *The Natural History*, c. AD 77–79

FOR HOT EYES AND RED

Take slugs, such as when you touch them will turn like the pummel of swords, a dozen or sixteen, shake them first in a clean cloth, and then in another, and not wash them, then stamp them, and put three or four spoonfuls of Ale to them, and strain it through a dry cloth, and give it the partie morning and evening, first and last.

– *A Choice Manual,* 1653

sie wogs a...

.M.

Langs ...
dorgne tho...
Aon gspie...
dorgne.
aber man ...
als man ...
an den ...

Ain Kos...
ain...

R. flor ...
Cichorea. ...
ʒij. rad. ...
...
aa. ʒiij. ...
Cinr. ...
ʒj. mirob...
ʒij. ...
...
...
...
...

...n sind dreyerley arten, schwarze, graue
blaue die schwarzen sind die besten. ...
...; die blauen die schwächsten, aber

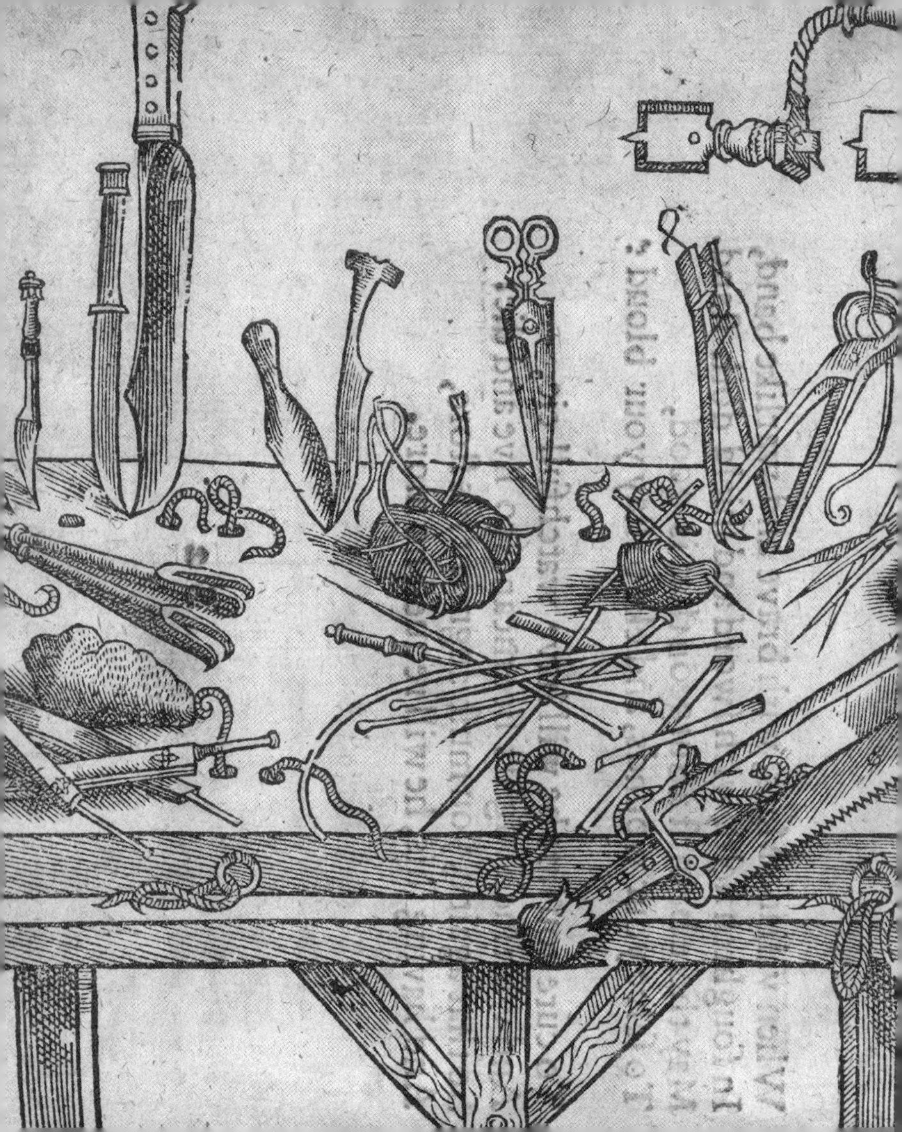

FOR HYDROPHOBIA CAUSED BY THE BITE OF A MAD DOG

The preventive cure consists in making deep scarifications, as soon as possible after the bite, in the part affected, and those adjacent to it; that they make a considerable discharge of blood, and apply large cupping glasses thereon; or it may be burnt pretty deep with an actual cautery. Then it should be made to suppurate by some corrosive application proper for that purpose; and during all that time it should be continually fomented with a pickle made with vinegar and salt; this should be continued for six months at least.

– *Encyclopaedia Britannica*, 1771

A MAGNETICK TRANSPLANTATION OF THE GOUT

Take of the hairs, and the pairings of the nails on the feet and hands of the Patient; bore a hole in an oke-tree to the pith; put them therein, and closing up the hole, cover it round about with Cow-dung, and within three months the Disease shall evanish.

– *Medicina Magnetica,* 1656

CURE FOR FELON AND CATARRH IN THE HAND

Take fourteen copper pennies and two pints of cider vinegar (have your vinegar right warm), then take seven of the pennies and heat them through, then drop them into the one pint and put your hand in as hot as you can bear it and leave it in until it becomes cool; then have the other pint ready with the other seven pennies and proceed in the same way until your hand is all wrinkled or shriveled. It generally affects a cure.

– *Everybody's Friend*, 1882

ANOTHER FOR BLEEDING AT THE NOSE

If a man bleed at the Nose, take a leathern point or lace, and tye it about his Testicles or Yard, and that will make the blood leave Mars, and run to look after Venus.

– *Culpeper's School of Physick*, 1659

CANCER ALE

Take Roots of Spanish Angelica, Burdock, Filipendula, each 4 ounces; Elecampane 2 Ounces; Gentian, Virginia Snakeroot, each 1 Ounce; Herb Robert, Ragwort, Sage, each 4 Handfuls; Scordium, Rue, each 2 Handfuls; live Millipedes 1 Pint; crude Antimony (broken into small Pieces, and tied up in a Rag) 1 Pound; put these in a Bag for 4 Gallons.

N.B. This Ale must, by no means be kept till stale and eager; and that not only upon account of the Millipedes, whose volatile Salt will be destroy'd by the Acid; but chiefly for the Sake of the Antimony, which, when unlocked by an Acid, is very inclinable to turn Emetic.

– *Pharmacopïa Extemporania*, 1730

DR. COFFIN'S,

California Medicines.

PAIN CEASES IMMEDIATELY!

THE
ELECTRIC NERVE PENCIL!

The Great Japanese Remedy.

Absolutely Annihilates the Severest Forms of HEADACHE, NEURALGIA, TOOTHACHE, RHEUMATISM, and Every Kind of NERVE PAIN in a Few Moments.

W. Boxford, June 24, 1884.

C. E. CARTER, Dear Sir:—It is with a great deal of pleasure that I can inform you of the benefit I have derived from the use of your wonderful "*Electric Nerve Pencil.*" I have been troubled with Nervous Headache for my whole life of fifty-four (54) years, and have never found any true relief until I used the *Electric Nerve Pencil*, it never fails to drive away the headache in less than five (5) minutes. I believe they are the only cure for this terrible malady, Nervous Headache. Yours, N. K. FOWLER.

Kittery, Me., Aug. 11, 1884.

C. E. CARTER. I have used your *Electric Nerve Pencil* for the toothache and headache, and I pronounce it the best thing out. It will cure every time. I would not take five dollars for mine if I could not get another.

Yours, GEO. O. WILSON.

FOR A COLD IN THE HEAD

A Compound Distillate of Creasote for inhaling from a handkerchief, and during sleep from the pillow. It has no similarity to other Creasotes, and must not be mistaken for them.

When Inhaled it has an immediate Curative effect on all the Respiratory Organs, as as it goes direct into the Lungs, it is absorbed by the Blood, and carried through the whole system, and its Curative effects continue all the time it is inhaled. It is a perfect, quick and certain Cure for Cold in the Head, Catarrh, Influenza, Sore Throat, Bronchitis, Asthma, Whooping Cough, Croup, Incipient Consumption, Hay Fever, &c., and all Diseases affecting the Breathing Organs. IT CURES TOOTHACHE LIKE MAGIC.

– British advertisement for Tottle's Pinol Creasote, 1901

A TRIED THING FOR THE CRAMP

Who use to rubbe their fingers betweene theyr toes of their feete when they go to bed, especially, when they smell most, and then to smell the same at their nose: it is a perfect remedy to put away the cramp. This was affyrmed to me as a tried thing.

– *A Thousand Notable Things,* 1579

THE CRAMP.

*Ecot! it's tied my foot in a Knot _ Oh!_Oh!_O_O_o_o_o_o_*

FOR THE EARS

Make a strong Decoction of Sage in the Urin of an healthy-Man, or of a Boy and with that sering the Ears, after which put into the Ear a small piece of the middle of a rosted Onion, and stop them up with black-Wool; repeat this sometimes if need requires.

– *The True Preserver and Restorer of Health*, 1695

Lord have Mercy upon us.

Death triumphant cloath'd in Ermine
'Bout whose bones do crawl the Vermine
Doth denote that each con[illegible]on
To his power must yeeld submission

5541

THE

Christians Refuge

OR

HEAVENLY ANTIDOT

against the

PLAGUE

In this time of Generall Contag

To which is added the

CHARITABLE PHYSICIA

Prescribing

Cheap and Absolute Remedie

For

PREVENTION and CUR

thereof

Published for the Benifit of

FAMILIES

Sold by *H. Marsh* at the Princes, Arm
in *Chancery-Lane* Price. 8 d. 166

AN APPROVED MEDICINE AGAINST THE PLAGUE

Amongst other excellent and approved Medicines against the Pestilence, there is none more available when the Sore appear, than to take a Cock, Pullet or Chicken, and pluck off the Feathers of the upper part of the Tail, till the Rump is bare; then hold the bare Rump to the Sore, and the Pullet will gape and struggle for Life, and at last will die with it then have another Pullet, and do the like to the Patient, and if that die, yet still apply the Patient with Pullets, so long as they die: for when the Poison is drawn away, the Chickens apply'd thereto will live; then the Sore presently abateth, and the Patient forthwith recovers.

– *The Housewife's Hospital,* 1717

OF THE HEDGE-HOG

Take the skin of the Hedge-Hog, and let it be made like a night-cap with the prickles, and put it on the sick bodies head, that therein is pained, it will procure him ease and make him sleep well.

– *Occult Physick,* 1660

DR JUNOD'S VACUUM APPARATUS

The object sought to be accomplished by the ingenious inventor is to determine a large portion of the blood of the system into the limb, and thus abstract it from congested or inflamed internal parts. This design he accomplishes by means of a tin boot, into which the leg of the patient is inserted, and from which the atmospheric air is gradually withdrawn, by means of a small air pump, the top of the boot being kept in air-tight apposition to the leg, by means of a broad belt of vulcanised india rubber … No pain, but only a slight uneasiness, is experienced in the limb enclosed in the boot, which is found, on being withdrawn, to be much increased in size.

– *The Journal of Health*, 1852

OPHTHALMIA

The right eye of a frog, suspended from the neck in a piece of cloth made from wool of the natural colour, is a cure for ophthalmia in the right eye; and the left eye of a frog, similarly suspended, for ophthalmia in the left.

– Pliny the Elder, *The Natural History*, c. AD 77–79

Augen Pulver
Augen Wasser
Augen Confect

TO MAKE OYL OF PUPPY, WHICH IS GOOD FOR ANY STRAIN OR BRUISE

Take a fat Spannell puppy, if you can get one, but let it be what puppy it will it must be fat, and dress him as you dress a pig, then take half a dose of yeolks of egges, and two handfuls of Roman nettles cut very small, three ounces of Venice turpentine, and three pennyworth of Saffron, and beat them altogether, and put them in the belly of the Puppy, and sow it up and roast it, and what droppeth from it save, and it will become perfect oyl for the former uses.

– *The Poor Man's Physician and Chyrurgion*, 1656

ANOTHER FOR CANCER

The moment cancer is discovered, dissolve ten grains of corrosive sublimate in a gill of whiskey, or a gill of strong spirit of any kind. Apply cautiously this mixture to the affected part; it may be done by making a small rag swab, wetting it with the solution just named, and touching the affected or sore part with it very gently. This operation is to be performed once a day, until the cancer is destroyed. This is a powerful remedy, and the pain produced by its application is very severe; but by an early application of this remedy, and bearing the pain of its application fifteen or twenty minutes for a few days, it will kill the cancer.

– *Gunn's Domestic Medicine*, 1830

Vitriol.
Alb.

Ocul.
Cancr.

AGAINST PHTHISICK [TUBERCULOSIS]

Take fresh Snails with their shells, in number Forty; cleanse them with a Linnen Cloath, then each of them being run through with a Bodkin; let the Apertures of the shells be fill'd with Powder of Sugar Candy, and being put in a Linnen Bag, let them be hung up in a Cellar, and let a Glass Vessel be set under them to receive the Syrup which will drop from them: The Dose of this is a spoonful twice or thrice a day in a fit Vehicle, viz. Aqua lactis, or some Pectoral Decoction.

– *The London Practice of Physick, Or The Whole Practical Part of Physick*, 1685

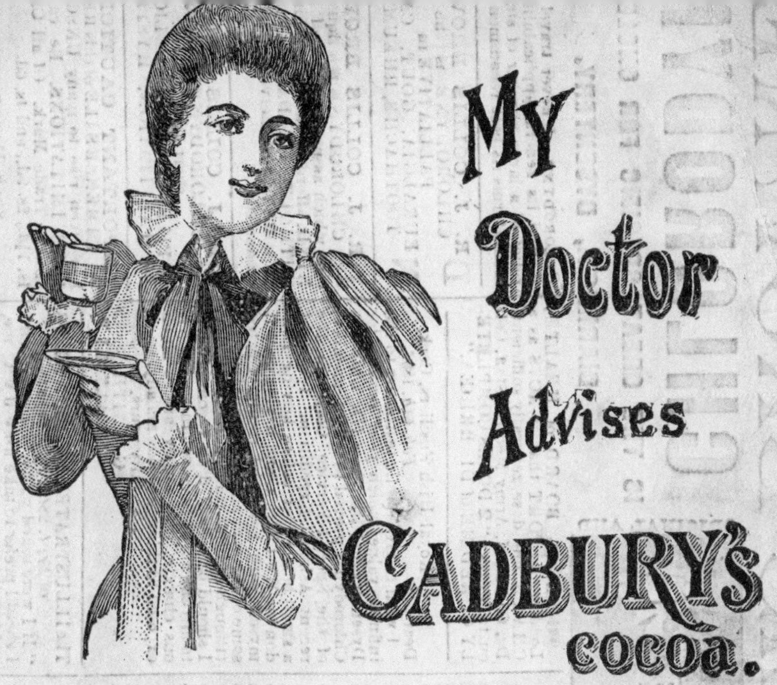
My Doctor
Advises
CADBURY'S
cocoa.

Because

It is Absolutely Pure.

It is free from Drugs and Chemicals.

It is a Perfect Food.

CADBURY'S Cocoa is very easily digested ; it imparts new life and vigour to those of delicate constitution, and can be safely and beneficially taken at all times and seasons.

TOOTHACHE

If a person rinses his teeth three times a year with blood of tortoises, he will be always exempt from toothache.

– Pliny the Elder, *The Natural History*, c. AD 77–79

TO RESTORE EYESIGHT

Let there be an occasional pressure of the finger on the ball of the eye. Let the pressure always be from the nose and towards the temples, and wash the eyes three times a day, in cold water. If this simple advice is followed, the day is not far distant when partial blindness shall disappear from the world.

– *Young's Great Book of Secrets*, 1873

MAYER, MERKEL & OTTMANN, LITH. 23 & 25 WARREN ST. N.Y.

CRÉME TERAS ROSA
THE BEST
FOR THE
COMPLEXION

CHAPTER

II

ALL IS VANITY

On beautifying the complexion, hair and figure

FOR CHAPT LIPS

Rub them with the sweat behind your eares, and this will make them smooth and well coloured.

– *A Rich Closet of Physical Secrets*, 1653

PIMPLE OINTMENT

Take 6 drachms of mercury, 6 grains of flour of sulphur, 2 ounces of hogs-lard; mix carefully in a mortar.

– *The Ladies' Guide to Beauty*, 1860

ARTIFICIAL EYELASHES

A Frenchman has discovered a means of planting artificial eyelashes and eyebrows.

The former operation is especially painful. A hair from the subject's head is threaded into a very fine needle, and a neat row of stitches is then made on the border of the eyelid.

The loops thus made are separated with scissors, leaving a row of lashes, which are pressed with an iron. A similar operation, somewhat less painful, is performed on the brows, and the transformation is complete.

– *The Hull Daily Mail,* 17 July 1908

WHAT WILL HE DO WITH IT?

Shampoo with **PACKER'S ALL-HEALING TAR SOAP,** *an astonishing remedy for Baldness, Dandruff, Skin Diseases &c. A perfect luxury for the Nursery, Toilet & Bath.*

Price, 25 Cents From Druggists.

THE PACKER MANUFACTURING CO.,
100 Fulton St., New York.

TO REMOVE HAIR FROM THE NOSTRILS

Take some very fine and clean wood ashes; dilute them with a little water, and with the finger rub some of the mixture within the nostrils. The hair will be removed without causing the least pain.

– *The Toilette of Health, Beauty and Fashion,* 1832

A SHRIVELED UP CREATURE!

Dry as a bunch of herbs, face like parchment, hair in thin whisps, hands skinny and bony, a long, thin lipped mouth, eyes small and red, the whole constituting an amalgamation of the cat and the ferret. This uninviting specimen of femininity was brought to this deplorable condition through using poisonous beautifying lotions and deadly cosmetics, in the vain endeavor to acquire what nature had denied her – a clear skin and healthy complexion. Had this unfortunate woman invested but one-twentieth part of her outlay in DR. CAMPBELL'S 'LIFE RENEWING' ARSENIC COMPLEXION WAFERS, the probabilities are that her portrait to-day would be as ATTRACTIVE as it now is HIDEOUS and REVOLTING. And yet she is but 40 years of age. Take WARNING ye who are following in the same ruinous and beauty destroying path.

By mail $1. Depot 220 Sixth av., New York. Sold by druggists.

– Advertisement in *The Decorator and Furnisher*, 1 September 1899

A PERFECT LOOKING NOSE

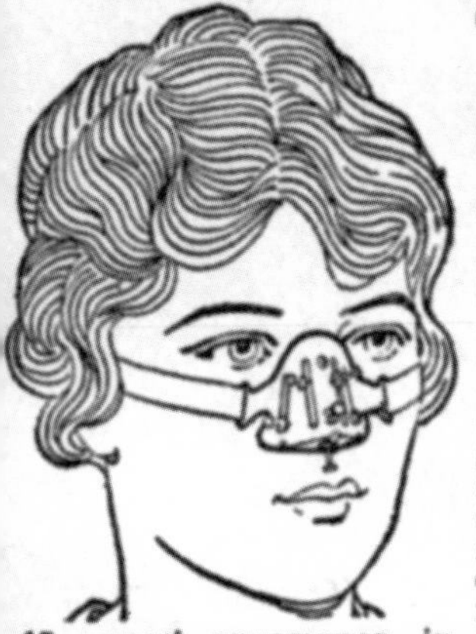

CAN EASILY BE YOURS.

Trados Model No. 25—British Patent—corrects all ill-shaped noses quickly, painlessly, permanently and comfortably at home (diseased cases excepted). It is the only adjustable, safe and guaranteed patent device that will actually give you a perfect looking nose. Over 89,000 satisfied users (ladies, gentlemen and children). For years recommended by physicians. 17 years' experience in manufacturing Nose Shapers is at your service. Write for free booklet which tells you how to obtain a perfect looking nose

M. TRILETY, ***Specialist,*** **Rex House, D.542, 45, Hatton Garden, London, E.C.1.**

THE NOSE MACHINE

This is a simple and successful contrivance which, applied to the nose for an hour daily, so directs the soft cartilage of which the member consists, that an ill-formed nose is quickly shaped to perfection. Any one can use them, and without pain. Price 10s. 6d., sent carriage free.—ALEX. ROSS, 248 High Holborn, London. Pamphlet sent for two stamps.

– Advertisement in *The Examiner* (London), 10 February 1872

ESAULINE

Every young man can positively and speedily cultivate a HEAVY, HANDSOME MOUSTACHE by a few applications of 'ESAULINE or POMADE D'ESAU,' the newly discovered Hair-forcing specific. Success guaranteed. Will not stain or injure the most delicate skin. Post free (under plain covers), 1s 3d., 2s 9d., and 5s.

– Advertisement in the *Penny Illustrated Paper* (London), 20 July 1895

GRECIAN WATER FOR DARKENING THE HAIR

Dissolve two drachms of nitrate of silver in 6 ounces of distilled water; perfume it to the taste, and wet the hair which is to be changed. If this touches the skin it will turn it black; though it does darken the hair at first, the black colouring will sometimes become purple.

– *The Ladies' Guide to Beauty*, 1860

REDUCE YOUR FLESH

You can safely and speedily reduce your superfluous flesh in any part of the body and thus improve your figure, by wearing DR. WALTER'S Famous Medicated Rubber Garments FOR MEN AND WOMEN. Neck and Chin Bands… $3.00. Chin only… $2.00. Also Union Suits, Stockings, Jackets, etc., for the purpose of reducing the flesh anywhere desired. Invaluable to those suffering from rheumatism.

– Advertisement in *The Theatre* magazine (US), March 1911

THE "VERY THING" FOR LADIES
FOR AN ELEGANT FIGURE & GOOD HEALTH
HARNESS' MAGNETIC CORSETS
PRICE ONLY 5/6 POST FREE
HARNESS MAGNETIC CORSET.
C.B. HARNESS
THEY CURE WEAK BACK.
FOR WOMEN OF ALL AGES.
HARNESS' MAGNETIC CORSETS
ONLY 5/6 POST FREE
By wearing these perfectly designed Corsets the most awkward figure become graceful and elegant, the internal organs are speedily strengthened,
THE CHEST IS AIDED IN ITS HEALTHY DEVELOPMENT.
And the entire system is invigorated.
Send at once Postal Order or Cheque for 5s. 6d. to the Secretary, C Dept.
THE MEDICAL BATTERY CO., LIMITED.
ONLY 5/6 POST FREE
52, OXFORD St. LONDON. W.
REGD. DESIGN.
P.T.O.

Beautys Lot.

Adorn'd with Tates, I well could Boast, Of Tons and Macaronys Toast;
I once was Fair, Young, Frisky, Gay, Could please with songs and Dance the Hay.
Dear Bells reflect Ye Mortals see, As I now am, so You will be.

Pub. as the Act directs by Wm. Humphrey 227 Strand London

PRINCESSES POWDER

It is with just Reason that this Powder has the Name of Princesses Powder, since four Princesses whose Beauty is so much talked of in Europe, are served with it, with so great Success, that by means of it, they have preserved their Skin, and their Beauty with an Air of Youth, till Seventy Years of Age. Madam de Montespan with whom the King of France has been so much in Love, very well knew, by this little Artifice, how to please that Prince, who has made her Beauty famous over all the habitable Earth; though naturally Madam de Montespan has no fine nor delicate Skin, but by the means of this Powder, which she has used all her life; she has preserved the fineness and Delicateness of her Skin so, that she does not appear above eighteen or twenty years of Age, though she be above fifty five.

– Advertising handbill, 1695

A SECRET TO TAKE AWAY WRINKLES

Heat an Iron Shovel red hot, throw on it some Powder of Myrrh, and receive the smoke on your face, covering the head with a napkin to prevent its being dissipated. Repeat this operation three times, then heat the shovel again, and when fiery hot pour on it a mouthful of White Wine. Receive the vapour of the Wine also on your face, and repeat it three times. Continue this method every night and morning as long as you find occasion.

– *The Toilet of Flora*, 1779

A KING
A BEAUTY
A BEGGAR
A WITCH

FLAGGING BREASTS

If a Woman annoint often her Dugges or Pappes with the iuyce of Succorie [juice of chicory], it will make them little, round and hard. For if they be hanging or flagging, it wyl draw them together, whereby they shal seeme as the Dugges of a mayde.

– *A Thousand Notable Things*, 1579

HAIR REMOVAL BY ANTS' EGGS

Take Gum of ivy, one ounce. Ants' eggs, Gum arabic, orpiment, of each one drachm. Reduce these to a fine powder, and make it up into a liniment, with a sufficient quantity of vinegar. In pounding the materials, great precaution must be taken that the dust of the orpiment, which is a preparation of arsenic, be not inhaled.

The formic acid, or acid of ants, may be more easily procured at the chemist's, and will answer the purpose better than the ants' eggs, which are not to be had at all seasons.

– *The Toilette of Health, Beauty and Fashion,* 1832

This is my appearance after a good dose of ARSENIC taken <u>medicinall</u>

MME A. RUPPERT'S FACE BLEACH

Lovely complexions. Clear, white skin.

Nothing will CURE, CLEAR and WHITEN the SKIN as quickly and permanently as Madame A. Ruppert's World-Renowned Face Bleach.

FACE BLEACH is not a new, untried remedy, but has been used by the best people for years, and for dissolving and removing FOREVER tan, SUNBURN, Moth, FRECKLES, Sallowness, BLACKHEADS, Eczema, PIMPLES, Redness etc., and bleaching, brightening and beautifying the complexion it has no equal.

– Advertisement in *Metropolitan Magazine*, 1895

INTERESTING TO LADIES

FAT-IL-GO
For Tightening Up Loose Flesh
Fat Melts Away Where It Is Used

DIRECTIONS
Pour in saucer, wet the fingers and rub in the parts to be treated.

For double chin do likewise, and sop on Fat-il-go with a cotton or sponge and let dry.

For a very fat neck it is advisable to wet a piece of cheese cloth with Fat-il-go and place inside of a chin strap and tie up the chin. It will reduce the flesh and leave the skin in perfect condition. Can be used frequently with surprising results. Delivered anywhere, $2.25 per bottle.

– Advertisement in *The Theatre* magazine (US), June 1911

CURVES OF YOUTH

will be yours if you will

"Pull the Cords"

Gives the Flesh the Resiliency and Freshness of Youth

Prevents Double Chins

Effaces Double Chins

Reduces Enlarged Glands

PROF. MACK'S

Chin Reducer and Beautifier

The only mechanism producing a concentrated, continuous massage of the chin and neck, dispelling flabbiness of the neck and throat, restoring a rounded contour to thin, scrawny necks and faces, bringing a natural, healthy color to the cheeks, effacing lines and wrinkles. Price only $10.

EDWARDS'
"HARLENE" FOR THE HAIR
THE GREAT HAIR DRESSING.
Restores the Hair.
Promotes the Growth.
Arrests the Fall.
Strengthens the Roots.
Removes Dandruff.
Beautifies the Hair.
Under Royal Patronage.

TO NOURISH THE HAIR

Beef marrow applied moderately to the hair of the head nourishes it, and communicates to it a fine gloss, as may frequently be seen among butchers, who often apply it. Whatever therefore nourishes, strengthens. The marrow also gives it a disposition to curl.

– *The Toilette of Health, Beauty and Fashion,* 1832

TO REDUCE LARGE BREASTS

Many ladies who are not troubled with general obesity of the system, have a superabundant development of the breast; the modern mode of reducing this is by a preparation of iodine but as this is a dangerous internal medicine in unprofessional hands, we shall recommend its external use, thus: Take Iodine of zinc,—1 drachm, Hog's lard,—1 ounce; mix well, and rub daily into each breast a piece about the size of a nutmeg, a linen bandage so placed as gently to compress the breast, without pressing on the nipple, will assist its operation.

– *The Ladies' Guide to Beauty*, 1860

FOR ANOINTING THE FACE

Galls of Bulls dry them gently in the Sun, afterward pour upon them Spirit of Wine, and draw forth a Tincture, which will be a little red, anoint the Face with this Tincture, and leave it on for three or four days, yet so, as the party, whose Face is so anointed, neither go out a dores, or freely expose her self to the Air. The time being elapsed, the Face must be often washed with Water of Bean-flowers, or of Nenuphar, or Polyginatum, also before anointing the Face may be well washt, with the same Waters, so, almost to a Miracle the Skin of the Face, and Neck, is rendred most gratefully white, delicate, and amiable.

– *Bazilica chymica, & Praxis chymiatricae,* 1670

mox vesicam cum liquore vel manu et liquore
infundat et si contingat obstaculum in ventre
interioris liquoris impediens ut saepius fit
pus continens tunc per sedem fistula
et vesicam comprimat et
concutiat liquorem interius
et tunc totum liquorem infundat. Quo infuso fiat pati-
ente iacente supinum i. ge-
nibus super lectum et fricet ventrem super um-
bilicum cum manu propria vel aliena. Et quando
poterit contineri clistere retineat. Et quando
minus retinere non valeat ad sellam vad-
at propriam cum pelvi obstante et ibi negoti-
a sua faciat. Et videat medicus egestiones ut
congnoscat si sanguinis vel putredo fiat an
unde sint egestiones indurata vel cola
cum fine saniei et si potest medicus
certificari quid in quodlibet casu sit agen-
dum. Clistere hoc est proprie notandum
quod quando medicus aliquem clistere admini-
strat si in fundendo liquorem cum clistere
quod tam cito gelet super manus medici

CHAPTER

III

EMBARRASSING BODIES

Of nether regions, errors of digestion, and unwholesome indiscretions

CHAFING

Riding on horseback, we well know, galls and chafes the inside of the thighs: the best remedy for accidents of this nature is to rub the parts with the foam which collects at a horse's mouth.

– Pliny the Elder, *The Natural History*, c. AD 77–79

A CERTAIN AND SIMPLE CURE FOR PILES

Take 8 cigars; rub them fine.
1 handful the inner bark of elder.
1 gill hog's lard.

Boil all the above ingredients together, and, after it becomes cool, anoint the part a few times a day.

– *Standard Cyclopedia of Recipes*, 1901

WORMS

If any be troubled with Stomach Worms, let him hold a piece of an honey-comb in his mouth, and the Worms will come out to the honey.

– *Culpeper's School of Physick*, 1659

BROWN'S VERMIFUGE COMFITS

OR

WORM LOZENGES

FOR THE FIRST SYMPTOMS OF THE POX

Obtain from any doctor's shop, a small quantity of Lunar Caustic; cut the end of a quill, and set the caustic into it, which will afford you an opportunity of using it more conveniently, and without handling it with your fingers; wet the end of this Caustic in water, and touch the chancres or sores with it lightly, twice a day, until you have killed the poison, always taking care to wash and cleanse the sores well with soap and water, immediately before this operation is performed.— The caustic will sting you a little; but never mind this; you are now on the stool of repentance, and are only learning the salutary moral lesson, that 'the penalty always treads upon the heels of the trangression,' and that the sacred laws of nature and her God, can never be violated without punishment to reform the offender!

– *Gunn's Domestic Medicine,* 1836

A BOTTLE OF HUNGARY WATER

Nolet, surgeon to the King of France and Marize Hospital at Brest, relates the following curious case: A monk wishing to get rid of a violent colic, introduced into the rectum a bottle of Hungary water (these bottles are generally long), through the cork of which he had made a small opening, to permit the fluid to flow into the intestine. In his anxiety to perform the operation well, he pushed the bottle so far that it completely entered into the gut. He could neither go to stool nor receive a lavement. A sage femme failed to insert her hand; the forceps and speculum were tried in vain; however, a boy, from eight to nine years of age, succeeded in introducing his hand and removed the bottle.

– *A Collection of Remarkable Cases in Surgery*, 1857

OFFENSIVE ODOURS OF THE MOUTH

To impart sweetness to the breath, it is recommended to rub the teeth with ashes of burnt mouse-dung and honey: some persons are in the habit of mixing fennel root. To pick the teeth with a vulture's feather, is productive of a sour breath; but to use a porcupine's quill for that purpose, greatly strengthens the teeth.

– Pliny the Elder, *The Natural History*, c. AD 77–79

AN EXCELLENT REMEDY FOR THE PILES

Another remedy, the conceit of which pleases me very well, is this; Take a gray Cat, and cut her throat, then flea her and roast her, and save her grease, boil the blood and the grease together, and anoint the Piles with it as hot as you can endure it; this seems to me pretty rational, because a Cat is a Beast of Saturn.

– *Culpeper's School of Physick*, 1659

USE THIS!
SWAYNE'S OINTMENT
SWAYNES OINTMENT
THE GREAT CURE.
FOR ITCHING PILES
& ALL
SKIN DISEASES
Why suffer longer from Itching Piles?
Why be longer annoyed by a trouble-
some Skin Disease? use
SWAYNE'S OINTMENT,
and you will be
cured.

A TAPEWORM TRAP

The object of my invention is to effect the removal of worms from the system, without employing medicines, and thereby causing much injury.

My invention consists in a trap which is baited, attached to a string, and swallowed by the patient after a fast of suitable duration to make the worm hungry. The worm seizes the bait, and its head is caught in the trap, which is then withdrawn from the patient's stomach by the string which has been left hanging from the mouth, dragging after it the whole length of the worm.

– US Letters Patent No. 11,942 – Alpheus Myers,
14 November 1854

A VERY GOOD MEDICINE TO CAUSE ONE TO PISSE THAT CANNOT

Take Horse-dounge out of the stable, new Butter & Aqua-vitae, of ech of them equall porcions, & frye them all together, and make thereof a Plaister, and applye it to the patient, from the Navill, to the Fundament, as hote as ever he may possibilie suffer it: But let not the Patient be afraide, although it cause bloud to issue foorth, for such is the nature of the Medicine, Also it causeth the Stone speadily to avoide.

– *A Rich Store-house or Treasury for the Diseased*, 1596

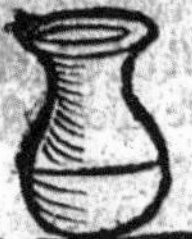

Albus color vt aqua fontis:

Glaucus color vt cornu lucidũ

Lacce9 color vt ſerum lactis.

Caropos color: vt vellus cameli.

Subpallidus color vt ſuccus carnis ſemicoctus non remiſſe.

Remiſſus pallidus vt ſucc9 carnis ſemicoct9 remiſſi.

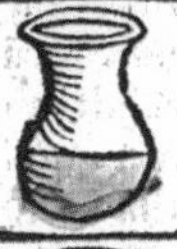

Subcitrinus vt pomi ſubcitrini non remiſſus

Citrin9 color vt pomi citrini remiſſi.

Subruffus color vt aurum remiſſum.

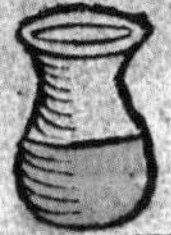

Subrubicũdus color vt croc9 occidentalis.

Rubeus vt crocus orientalis.

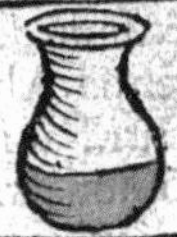

Subrubicũdus vt flãma ignis remiſſa.

Rubicundus vt flãma iguis nõ remiſſa.

Inops color vt epatis animalis.

Kyamos color: vt vinum bene nigrum.

Viridis color vt caulis viridis.

Liuid9 color vt plumbum.

Niger vt incauſtum.

CONSTIPATION

Constipation can be cured by the INTERNAL BATH.
THE EAGER INTESTINE CLEANSER AND IDEAL VAGINAL DOUCHE (a syringe operated by weight of the body) gives immediate relief without medicine, washing your intestines clean.
You want the best. Investigate before buying. Our cleanser has special appliances all its own. The activity of the Large Intestine, is all important to Health. Compel it to perform its duty by Internal Bathing and Prevent Disease.

– Advertisement in *The World Almanac,* 1920

A SMEARING FOR A PENETRATING WORM

Take swines gall, and fishes gall and crabs gall, and hares gall; mingle them together, smear the wounds therewith; blow with a reed the liquid into the wound; then pound hart bramble leaves, lay them on the wounds.

– *The Lacnunga*, 10th-century England

OF THE FALLING DOWN OF THE FUNDAMENT

If the Gut be sunk down, anoint it with Oyl of Rose and Myrtle, mixing a little powder of Galls amongst it, and with your Fingers and a small Linnen-Rag, put it in. …

There is yet another, though in appearance ridiculous, yet in reality a good way of reducing the Gut. With a strong hand strike five or six times the Patient's Buttocks, and thereby the Muscles, called Ani levatores, will presently draw the Anus into its right place again. But before the Patient be thus chastized, take care that the Gut may first be anointed with Oyl of Roses, or of Myrtle.

– *Thesaurus chirurgiae: the chirurgical and anatomical works of Paul Barbette*, 1687

THE EFFECTS OF MERCURY TREATMENT FOR THE POX

After Three, Four, or Five Days, thus managed, we usually observe the Fauces to inflame, the Inside of their Cheeks to lie tumid or high and thick, being ready to fall in betwixt the Teeth, upon shutting of the Mouth; the Tongue looks white and foul, the Gums also stand out, the Breath stinks (which is a good Omen of its coming on), and in general the whole Inside of the Mouth appears shining, seems as it were parboil'd, lying in Furrows, much after the Manner as it does in those who have lately held strong Spirits therein for the Tooth-ach.

– Daniel Turner, *Syphilis*, 1717

PRACTICAL
SCHEME

FOR RECOVERING PERSONS APPARENTLY DROWNED

Blow with force into the lungs, by applying the mouth to that part of the patient, closing the nostrils with one hand, or rather thro' the nostrils, closing the mouth, and gently expelling the air again by pressing the chest with the other, imitating the strong breathing of a healthy person; the medium of a handkerchief or cloth may be used to render the operation less indelicate.

Whilst one assistant is constantly employed in this operation, another should throw the smoke of tobacco up by the fundament into the bowels, by means of a pipe or fumigator; a pair of bellows may be used until the others can be procured.

– Recommendations of Chester Infirmary, printed in the *Chester Chronicle*, 22 November 1776

A THREAD OF LINEN

To arrest incontinence of urine, the extremities of the generative organs should be tied with a thread of linen or papyrus, and a binding passed round the middle of the thigh.

– Pliny the Elder, *The Natural History*, c. AD 77–79

A BLOODY FLUX

One who had a Bloody Flux, with a pain in his Belly, had used many things, but all in vain: At length he sat over the fumes of a decoction of Beans, and took it in by straining, and thrusting forth his Fundament: He found nothing which did him more good.

– *Collectanea Medica*, 1703

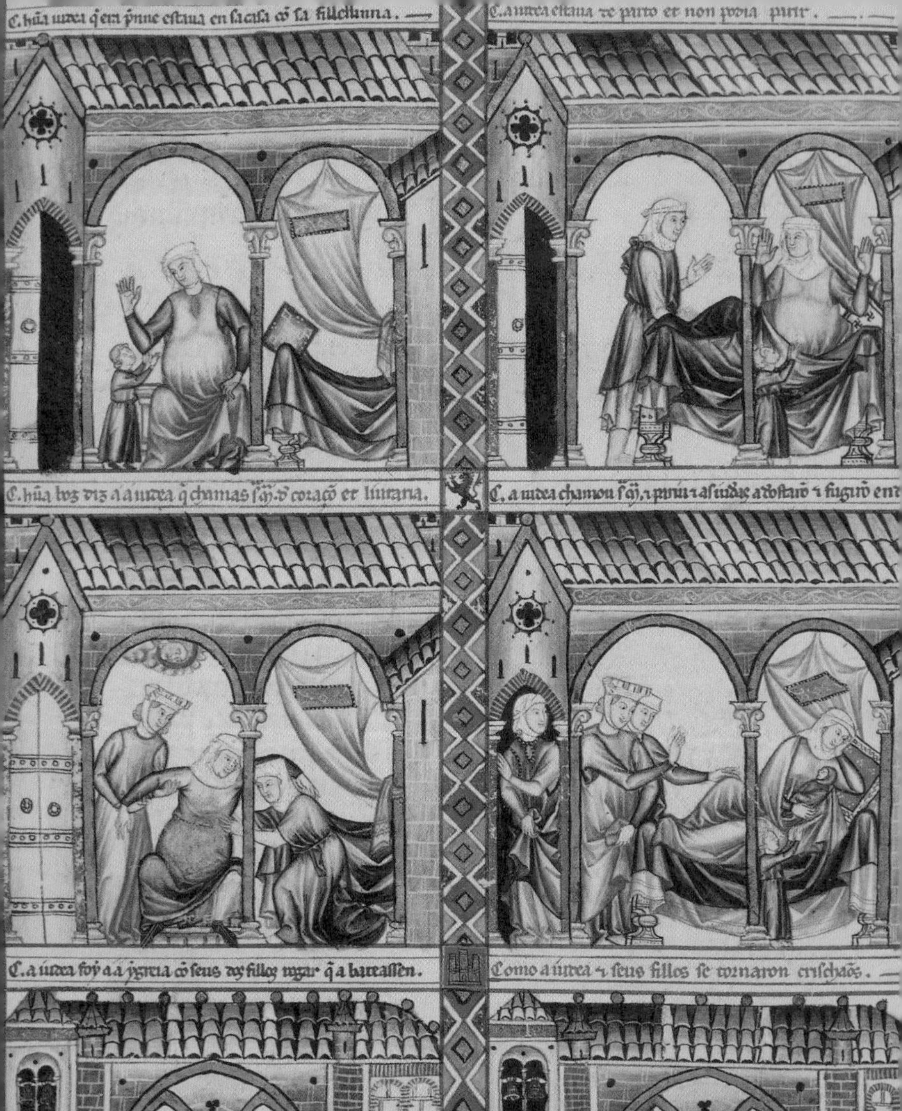

C. hũa iudea q̃ era ꝑnne estaua en sa casa cõ sa filletinna.
C. a iudea estaua de parto et non podia parir.
C. hũa boz diz a a iudea q̃ chamas s. m. d' coraçõ et liuraria.
C. a iudea chamou s. m. i pariu i as iudias a costaro i fugiro en
C. a iudea foy a a ygreia cõ seus dos fillos rogar q̃ a bateassen.
Como a iudea i seus fillos se tornaron crischaõs.

CHAPTER

IV

FAMILY MATTERS

On love, marriage and the patter of tiny feet

MAY'S CELEBRATED LOVE LOZENGES

Sure and safe, pleasant in taste, certain in effect; gain the undying love and affection of any one you wish; none can resist their magnetic influence. In boxes, post free, 9 stamps; extra strong, 18 stamps. The best are the cheapest. – Mr. MAY, Pharmaceutical Chemist (by diploma), 22, Heaton-road, Peckham-rye, London.

– Advertisement in *Reynolds's Newspaper* (London),
30 November 1873

A BALSAMICK ESSENCE

God the author of all things, to make Man in love with his Wife, in her state of Innocency, he made her smooth, soft, delicate and fair, to intice him to imbrace her; I therefore, that Women might be pleasing to their Husbands, and that they might not be offended at their Deformities, and turn into other Womens Chambers, do commend unto you the Virtue of an eminent and highly approved Balsamick Essence, with several other incomparable Cosmeticks, faithfully prepared without Mercury.

– Advertising handbill (London), 1675

'MENDELEJEN' BRAND GLANDULAR ELIXIR

An Austrian Specific for INABILITY and SEX-ATROPHY.

A new and wonderful type of medicine for threatened impotency in men, sex-quiescence and feminine passivity. A pleasant-tasting but powerful rejuvenating liquid mixture for both sexes of all ages and a marvellous neuro-spinal tonic and cure for impotency and sexual neurasthenia. Restores the vital energies to the old, middle-aged, or prematurely aged. Prepared from extracts of various glandular substances of interior secretion based on the scientific research of Viennese, French and Russian physiologists to stimulate the ductless glands, to assist the reproductive energy and renew exhausted tissue and recreative substance.

– Hancock & Co brochure, early 1900s

Elixir of Life
DROPS

THE DEAD STRIP

Girls have been known to go to a graveyard at night, exhume a corpse that had been nine days buried, and tear down a strip of the skin from head to foot; this they manage to tie round the leg or arm of the man they love while he sleeps, taking care to remove it before his awaking. And so long as the girl keeps this strip of skin in her possession, secretly hidden from all eyes, so long will she retain the man's love.

– *Ancient Cures, Charms and Usages of Ireland*, 1890

AN AMULET

The teeth of the right jaw of the amphibious crocodile, attached to the right arm as an amulet, acts as an aphrodisiac, that is, if we choose to believe it.

– Pliny the Elder, *The Natural History*, c. AD 77–79

LOVE'S REWARD

BE A MAN

Throw Away Your Medicine – Our VACUUM ORGAN DEVELOPER WILL RESTORE YOU.
NO CURE, NO PAY.
Our Vacuum Organ Developer should be used by every man. It cures where everything else fails and hope is dead. It restores small, weak organs, lost power, failing manhood, drains, errors of youth, etc. Stricture or Variocele permanently cured in 1 to 4 weeks.

No drugs to ruin the stomach. No Electric Belts to blister and burn. Our Vacuum Developer is a local treatment applied directly to the weak and disordered parts. It gives strength and development wherever applied.

– Advertisement in the *Minneapolis Journal,*
9 November 1901

AGAINST SORCERY

If a marryed man bee let or hyndered through Inchauntment, Sorcery or Witchcraft, from the acte of generation, let him make water through his maryage Ring, and he shalbe lowsed from the same, and their doinges shall have no further power in him.

– *A Thousand Notable Things*, 1579

THE MORMON ELDERS' DAMIANA WAFERS

The Most Powerful Invigorant.
Permanently restores IMPOTENT MEN to PERFECT MANHOOD, SEXUAL POWER and PROCREATIVE ABILITY.

They cure every trace of DEBILITY, SPERMATORRHOEA, and every form of Seminal losses and weakness whether due to Youthful Folly, Abuse, or Natural Failure.

Damiana Wafers are a safe, certain, and speedy cure for nearly all varieties of seminal and physical debility of the generative organs of both sexes, endorsed by the medical faculty, and relied upon by the heads of the Mormon Church as a remedy for Nervous Debility, and all Weaknesses which would disqualify them as members of their faith.

– Advertisement in the *Canadian Pharmaceutical Journal*, 1885

A NETTLE

If a Woman desire to know whether she be with childe, or not, let her make water in a clean copper or brazen vessel at night when she goes to bed, and put a Nettle in it, if the Nettle have red spots in it next morning, she is with childe, else not.

– *Culpeper's School of Physick*, 1659

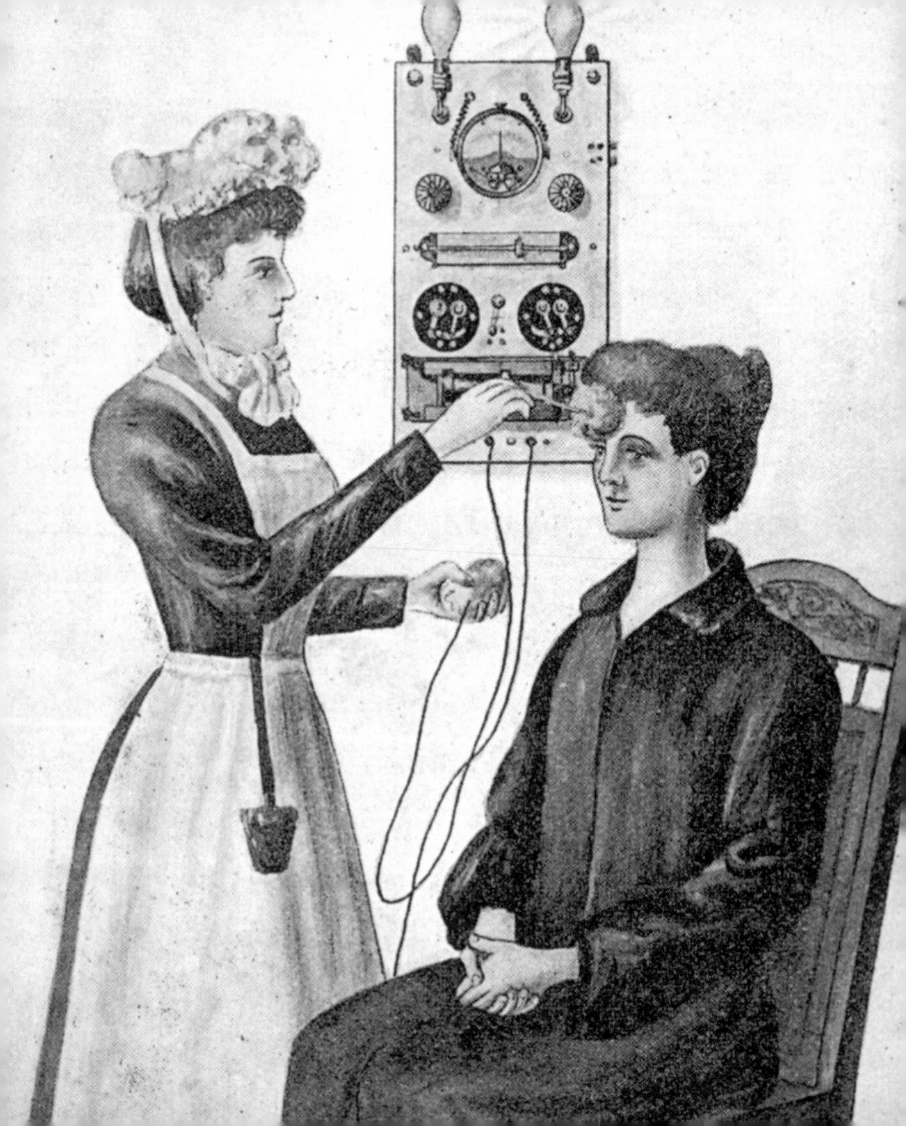

TO KNOW THE SOURCE OF BARRENNESS

Take a Handful of Barley (any other Corn that will quickly grow will serve the turn as well) and steep half of it in the Urine of the Man, and the other half in the Urine of the Woman, the space of four and twenty Hours, then take it out and set it, the Man's by itself, and the Woman's by itself, set it in a Flower-pot or something else where you may keep it dry, then Water the Man's every Morning with his own Urine, the Woman's with hers, and the which grows first is the greatest sign of Fruitfulness.

– Culpeper, *A Directory for Midwives,* 1652

A FROG

If a woman takes a Frog and opens his mouth, and spit in it thrice, she shall not conceive that year.

– *Occult Physick,* 1660

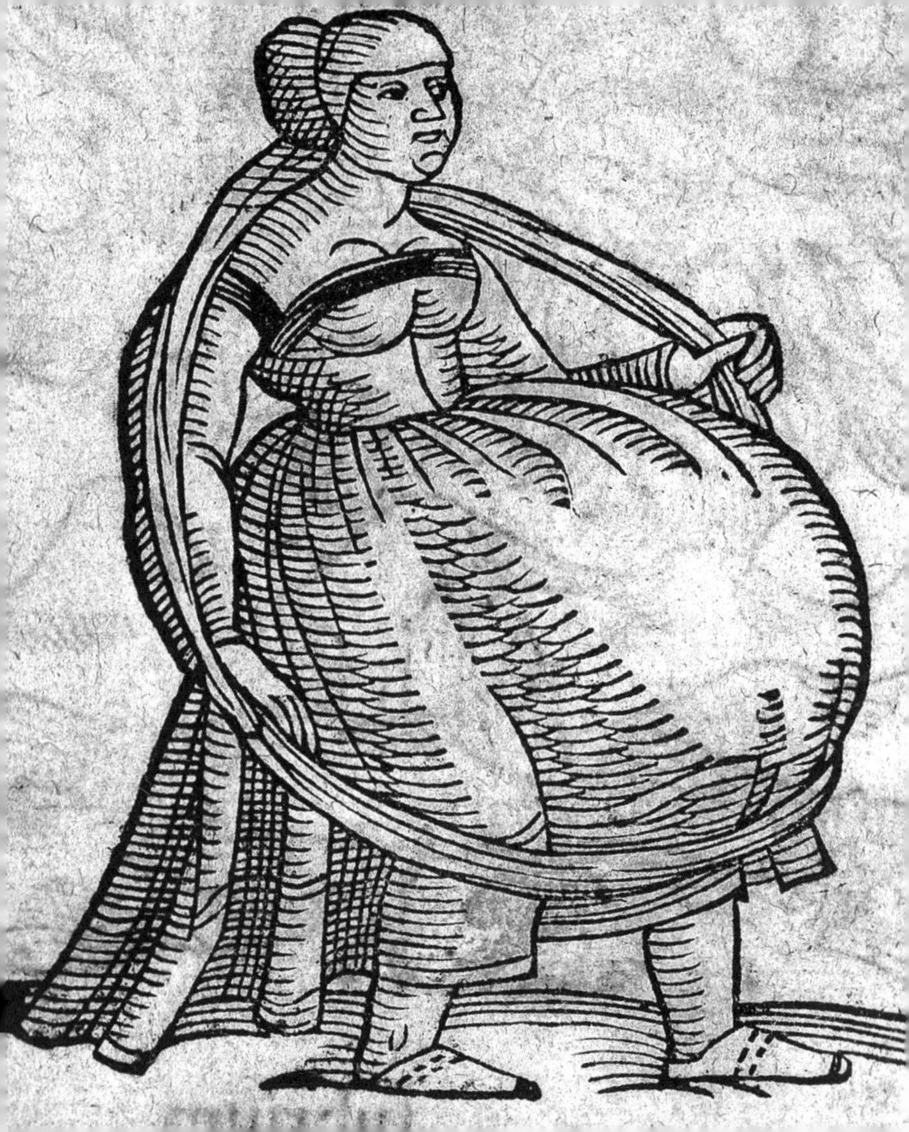

TO HASTEN CHILDBIRTH

Delivery, when near at hand, will be accelerated, if the man by whom the woman has conceived, unties his girdle, and, after tying it round her, unties it, adding at the same time this formula, 'I have tied it, and I will untie it,' and then taking his departure.

– Pliny the Elder, *The Natural History*, c. AD 77–79

ANOTHER FOR EASING DELIVERY

It is said, that if a person takes a stone or other missile which has slain three living creatures, a man, a boar, and a bear, at three blows, and throws it over the roof of a house in which there is a pregnant woman, her delivery, however difficult, will be instantly accelerated thereby.

– Pliny the Elder, *The Natural History*, c. AD 77–79

Ful solemply / there he was receyued
The contre glad / of his repeir a geyn
And aftir soone / Cilbaare hath conceyued
Thorugh goddis grace / that werkith neuer in veyn
And in that yeer / she bar a child certeyn
In Nozenberghes / a cite of gret fame
Of god prouided / Edmond was his name

TO EASE A WOMAN OF HER AFTER-PAINS

Take Tar and Barrows-grease, of each equal quantities, boil them together, and in boiling adde a little Pigeons-dung to it, spread some of it upon a linen cloth, and apply it to the back of a woman newly delivered, that is troubled with After-pains, and it will give her ease.

– *Culpeper's School of Physick*, 1659

CUTTING THE TEETH

The Gums of young children, being often rubbed with the brains of a Hare or Cunney, their teeth will cut easily.

– *Culpeper's School of Physick,* 1659

HORSFORDS ACID PHOSPHATE
FOR MENTAL & PHYSICAL
EXHAUSTION, DYSPEPSIA, &c

TEETHING

First put this famous Anodyne Necklace about the Child's Neck, to be WORN as common Necklaces are: Then from Time to Time let the Nurse, or Mother Rub the Child's Gums To and Fro with their Finger Wet in a little of the foregoing Pain-Easing Cordial, as above Directed, to allay the Pain, Anguish, & Inflammation of the Gums, and to soften them for the Teeth to come safely out, without the Necessity of Cutting the Gums, as is Many Times unwarily done, excepting in such, whose Gums are found to be extremely hard, or of a gristly Nature.

– Advertising handbill, 1725

A CURE FOR SCABBY HEADS ON CHILDREN

Take 1 pound pickled pork.
1 pound cabbage.
Boil the above the same as you would for eating; then skim it off, and wash the head with the liquid.

– *Standard Cyclopaedia of Recipes*, 1901

CHAPTER

V

TIRED AND EMOTIONAL

Melancholy, mania and addictive habits

MEANS OF RESTORING A DRUNKEN PERSON

Let the patient be placed in a chair, supporting his head, and then administer a wine glass full of the best vinegar, rubbing his temples gently with a little of the same. If the good effect be not seen in ten minutes, other means must be employed. If the patient is in the first stage of the fit, that is, if his face is red, and his skin hot, let him be stripped, and have a pail of water showered on him from three feet above his head. This may be repeated three or four times. If this does not produce a full effect, give thirty grains of ipecacuanha.

– *The Medical Adviser and Guide to Health and Long Life*, 1824

ore Lane. Eng.d

CHAMPAIGN DRIVING AWAY REAL PAIN.

Wine Cures the Gout, the Colic and the Phthisic.
Wine it is to all men the very Best of Physic.

Published by Thos. McLean 26 Haymarket, London 1827.

TO MAKE ONE LOATHE WINE

If Eeles be suffocated in wyne, whosoever shall drynke of that wyne, (though they have been very much geven to wyne before, & could scantly abstayne from the same,) they wyl loothe wyne, and not be desyrous to drinke wine after. The greene Frogges which use or leapes about sprynges, if they be suffocated in wyne, workes the lyke effect.

– *A Thousand Notable Things*, 1579

TREMBLING

A Super-super-excellent Paste for the shaking and trembling of the Hands after hard drinking, or otherwise; and it will make them Smooth, Soft, and of a delicate white Colour, although you were to scower Brass and Pewter, and make Coal-fires every day, yet no Body will imagine you do any such drudgery, as hundreds can testifie. Price One Shilling each Box.

– Advertising handbill (London), 1675

A CURE FOR MORPHINE ADDICTION

MORPHINE and other drug habits are positively cured by HABITINA. For hypodermic or internal use. Sample sent to any drug habitué by mail. Free. Regular price $2.00 per bottle at your druggist or by mail in plain wrapper.

– Advertisement, *The Fort Wayne Journal-Gazette,* 17 April 1907

From the label:
HABITINA contains 1% alcohol.
One fluid ounce contains:
16 grains morphine sulphate
8 grains diacetyl morphine hydrochloride (morphine derivative)
with other ingredients.

SA-TAN-IC LINIMENT

'For all the world'. It brings mental sunshine.

'How's your disposition?' is equivalent to asking 'How's your liver?' A fit of the 'blues' and a disordered liver go hand in hand. SA-TAN-IC makes you 'sunny' – goes right to the cause of the trouble – gives the liver and digestive organs a thorough toning. Result – improved digestion, better appetite, nourished nerves and cheerfulness. Try SA-TAN-IC as a 'flu' preventive. Also relieves colds, indigestion, rheumatism and most nervous troubles, and most headaches.

– US advertisement, 1920

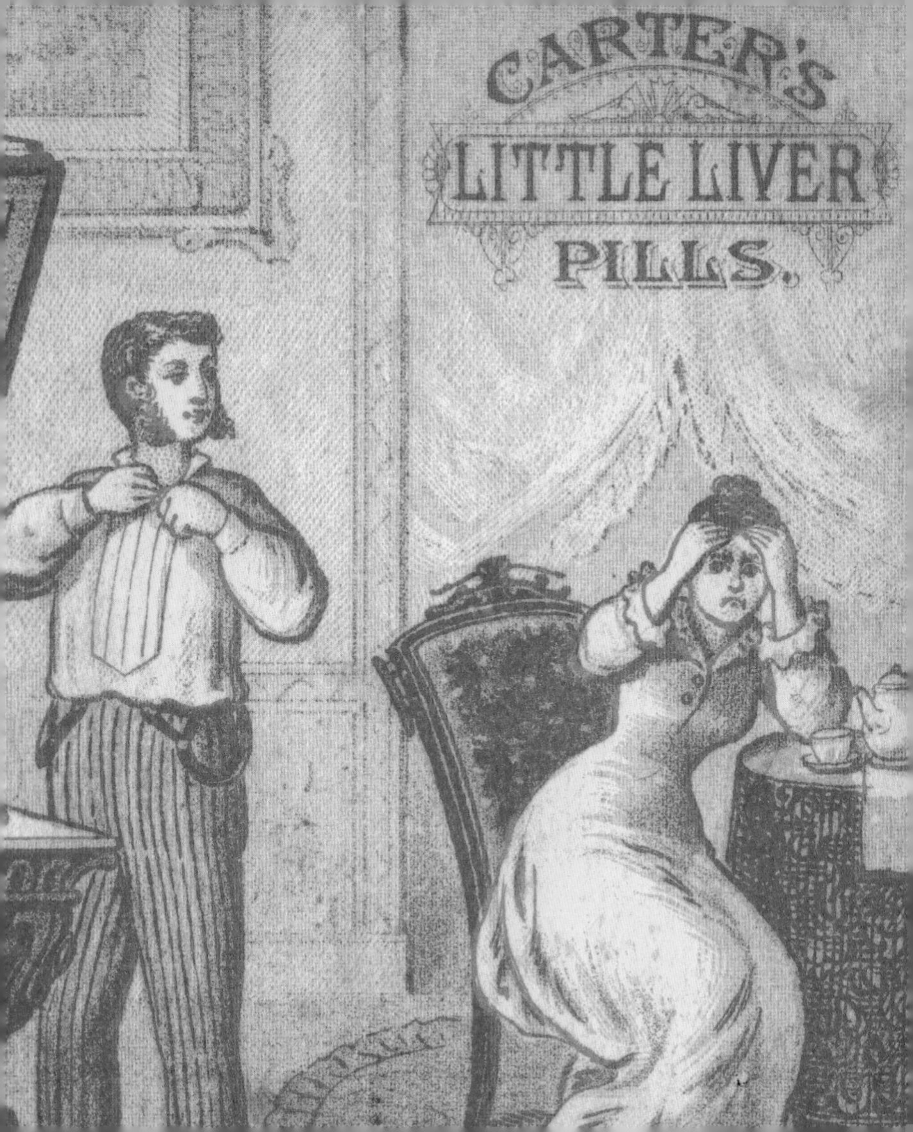
CARTER'S
LITTLE LIVER
PILLS.

THE SKIN OF A MERESWINE

In case a man be lunatic; take skin of a mereswine or porpoise, work it into a whip, swinge the man therewith, soon he will be well. Amen.

– *The Lacnunga*, 10th-century England

THE CURE OF LOVE-MELANCHOLY

It seemes to bee very necessary in the first place to take away the superfluity of Blood, by opening the Liver Veine in the right arme. And if the party be of a good Constitution, Sanguine, and well in flesh, you may take the greater quantity from him; because that their strength will bee able to beare the losse of the greater store of Blood.

– Jacques Ferrand, *Erotomania*, 1640

Nomen herbe. Cyclaminos. Omoeos. Celeron.
Alii. Anthion. Alii. Cassofillos. Alii. Chedonion. Zoro

AGAINST GOBLIN VISITORS

Work a salve against nocturnal goblin visitors; boil in butter lupins, hedgerife, bishopwort, red maythe, cropleek, salt; smear the man therewith, it will soon be well with him.

– *The Lacnunga*, 10th-century England

OVER-BRAINWORK

A Marvellous Remedy!! 'Brain Salt', the Specific for Headache and Sea-Sickness.

'Brain Salt' is not put forward as an universal remedy, but it is what its name indicates, viz., an Effervescing Medicinal Salt, for the cure or relief for the effects of over-brainwork. Used as directed, it brightens and refreshes the exhausted sufferer, to whom even temporary relief may have seemed an impossibility.

– English advertising handbill, 1879

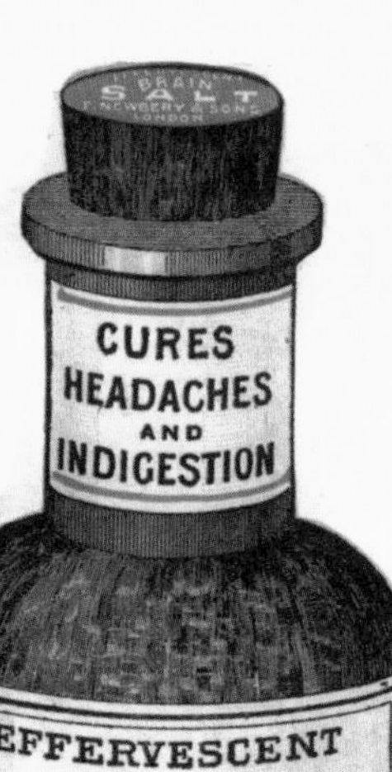
BRAIN
SALT
F. NEWBERY & SONS
LONDON
CURES
HEADACHES
AND
INDIGESTION
EFFERVESCENT
BRAIN
SALT
(TITLE REGISTERED) PRICE 2/9 PER BOTTLE
A POSITIVE RELIEF AND CURE FOR
Brain Troubles, Headaches
Sea Sickness,
Nervous Debility, Sleeplessness, Excessive Study, Mania, Over Brainwork,
etc etc.
F. NEWBERY & SONS.
1 and 3 King Edward St. London, E.C.
TRADE MARK REGISTERED IN U.S. BY F. NEWBERY & SONS. FEB 10 1888

ON LYCAEON, OR LYCANTHROPIA

Those labouring under lycanthropia go out during the night imitating wolves in all things, and lingering about sepulchres until morning …

You must know that lycanthropia is a species of melancholy which you may cure at the time of the attack, by opening a vein and abstracting blood to fainting, and dieting the patient with wholesome food. Let him use baths of sweet water, and then milk-whey for three days, and purging him with the hiera from colocynth twice or thrice. After the purgings, use the theriac of vipers, and administer those things mentioned for the cure of melancholy. When the disease is already formed, use soporific embrocations, and rub the nostrils with opium when they are going to rest.

– *The Medical Works of Paulus Aegineta*,
1st-century Greece

HYSTERICON, FOR FITS OF THE MOTHER

Hystericon, or Antidote against Fits, Vapours, Hypochondriack Melancholy, Vertigoe, Giddiness or Swimming in the Head, Phrenzy, or Deprivation of Senses, Suffocations, or Risings in the Throat, Faintings, Swoonings, &c. (commonly called Fits of the Mother) for all which, it's a most admirable thing for Prevention as well as Cure, whether the Cause be Suppression, or Stoppage of the Spleen, &c. or Hypochondriack, in admirably prevailing against, and taking away the very Cause of such Distempers, that they seldom return again; wonderfully comforts, relieves and cherishes Languishing Nature, restores and corroborates the weaken'd Faculties, revives the Spirits, and enlivens the whole Body, with so much Celerity, Ease, Safety, and Pleasure, that it has scarcely its Equal. Sold at Mr Stephens's in Broadstreet, near the Royal-Exchange, at 1s. 6d. a Bottle, with Directions.

– Advertisement, *A Review of the Affairs of France*, 12 April 1705

de gresse que les braceletz de sa femme luy seruoient d'anneaux a ses doigtz, comme les historiens escriuent. Comme

Histoire d'un Roy qui estoit si gras, quil se faisoit tirer sa graisse auecques des Sagsues.

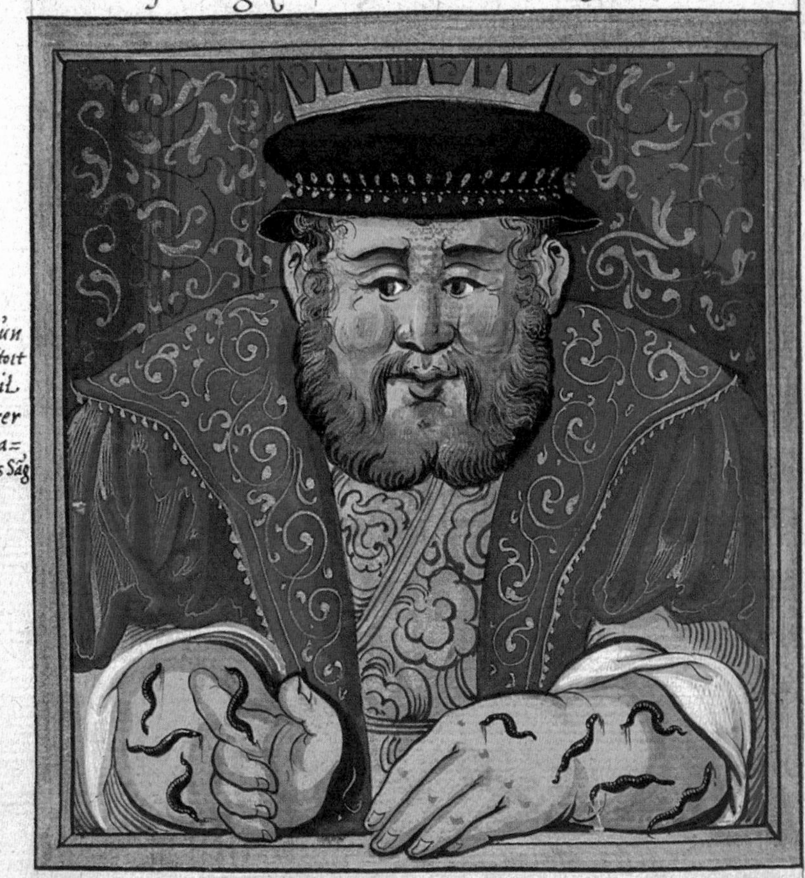

en semblable ce grand tirant Denis Heraclet se laissa si bien transporter a ses delices qu'il s'habitua en fin de ne

MELANCHOLY DISEASES

Leaches or bloudsuckers, are wormes found in waters, which applied outwardly to the member, draw forth bloud…

So oftentimes wee apply them to the Arse-hole called Anus, against melancholy diseases, caused of the stopping of hemorroids.

– *The English Phlebotomy*, 1592

SWINGING

This is both a moral and medical mean in the treatment of maniacs. It may be employed in either the oscillatory or common, or the circulating form. The first, or oscillatory, is too generally known to require a description: the second, or circulating, is easily constructed by suspending a common Windsor chair to a hook in the ceiling, by two parallel ropes attached to the hind legs, and by two others passing round the front ones joined by a sliding knot, that may regulate the elevation of the patient when seated, who, besides being secured in a strait waistcoat, should be prevented from falling out of the chair by a broad leather strap, passed round the waist and buckled behind to the spars, while another strap to each leg may fasten it to the front ones of the chair. The patient thus secured, and suspended a few inches from the ground; the motion may be communicated by an attendant turning him round according to the degree of velocity required.

– Joseph Mason Cox, *Practical Observations on Insanity*, 1806

Voyez pour la face latérale de la mécanique le dessin précédent.

MVNDIPRE
SENTIS SE
EXHIS FOR
MANTRQVE

LETHARGY

Persons are aroused from lethargy by applying to the nostrils the callosities from an ass's leg steeped in vinegar, or the fumes of burnt goats' hooves or hair, or by the application of a wild boar's liver: a remedy which is also used for confirmed drowsiness.

– Pliny the Elder, *The Natural History*, c. AD 77–79

THIS IS WHAT WE CALL THE COLD PILLIP SIR!

HYDROPATHY FOR HYPOCHONDRIA

First operation was to put him into a cold bath, and use strong friction for an hour. He was put into a packing-sheet, in which he became delirious; he was then rubbed by four men in a tepid bath 64°. He was still unconscious and yet winced on being pinched; water thrown on his head caused a slight cry; great heat on the head. On ceasing the cold affusion, pulse though oppressed begun to be felt – eyes fixed – conjunctiva inflamed.

– *Every Man His Own Doctor: The Cold-Water, Tepid-Water and Friction-Cure*, 1849

Von laſſen mit kopffen im bad.

As laſſen dz man thůt an
dem lyp vßwendig das iſ
gut wan man wirt dauon
nitt als kranck als von an
derm laſſen. Man ſol me
cken das vil ſtedt ſynd a

...o cui signum mit
...lauenieb. et cid
...gltipliatte ei no
...ia q i ydropi...
Et sicut diuisa
...ebra. ... diu
...iustitate significa
...stimonium. Ar
...ut et fame. Tau
...emum: huius
...Cane: Pect

Tercia gratia lacrimarum ma...
diuisitate materie. s. cu...
lio sirupo. deinde purget...
cum esula acuatis. In ca...
uel cum cattaritico spiriali. ...
Tercia acuista: cum enim...
tenuitatis. s. spacio. iij. die...
...tti a stupha uel cum d...
o libanum uel exhibicio th...
...tutam restringit lacrimas...
euitanda sunt debilitatiua...

...npositionibus, et necessitate.

De uermibus aurium et p(ro)pt(er) splend...

Duplicae co(n)tingit a...

...niari. aliq(uan)n(do) s(ecundu)m ...

...tu(m). angustiam cu(m) f...

...passio cu(m) magno i...

...to p(er) causa(m) ... Jn p(ri)mis